It's Easy To Play
Abba.

Wise Publications
London/New York/Sydney/Paris/Copenhagen/Madrid/Tokyo

Exclusive Distributors
Music Sales Limited
8/9 Frith Street, London W1V 5TZ, England
Music Sales Pty. Limited
120 Rothschild Avenue, Roseberry, NSW 2018 Australia

This book © Copyright 1983 by
Wise Publications
ISBN 0.7119.0340.9
Order No. AM22195

Cover Photograph courtesy of London Features International
Arranged by Frank Booth

Music Sales complete catalogue lists thousands
of titles and is free from your local music
book shop, or direct from Music Sales Limited.
Please send a Cheque or Postal Order for £1.50 for postage to
Music Sales Limited, 8/9 Frith Street, London W1V 5TZ.

Printed in England by
Caligraving Limited, Thetford, Norfolk

Knowing Me, Knowing You

Words and Music by Benny Andersson, Stig Anderson and Björn Ulvaeus

Steady 4

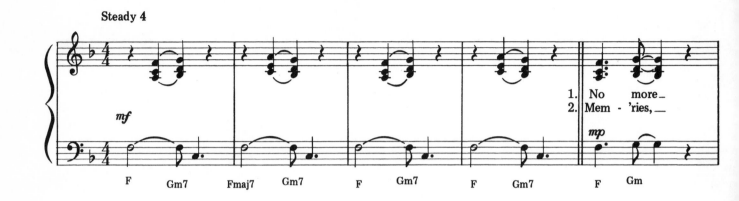

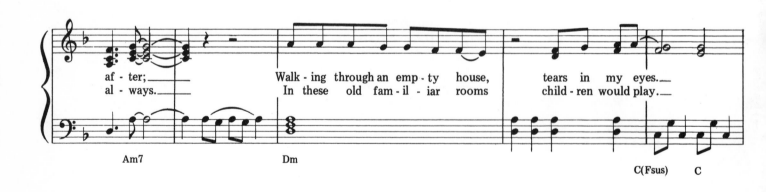

you,   there is no-thing we can   do, Know-ing me, know-ing you.

C   F   B♭ C

We just have to face it, this time   we're   through.   Break- in' up is nev - er

F   B♭   C   F   Am

To Coda ⊕

ea - sy, I know but I have   to   go.   Know-ing me, know-ing you, it's the

B♭   C7   F   B♭   C   F   B♭

D. % al Coda ⊕

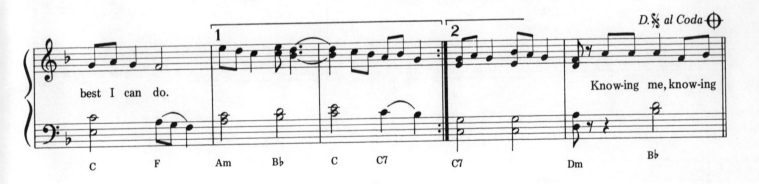

best I can do.   [1]   [2]   Know-ing me, know-ing

C   F   Am B♭   C C7   C7   Dm   B♭

Repeat and Fade

⊕ **CODA**

best I can   do.

C   F   Dm   Am   B♭   C7

Arrival

Music by Benny Andersson and Björn Ulvaeus

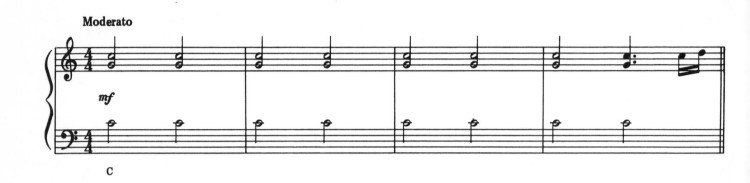

7

I Do, I Do, I Do, I Do, I Do,

Words and Music by Benny Andersson, Stig Anderson and Björn Ulvaeus

Take A Chance On Me

Words and Music by Benny Andersson and Björn Ulvaeus

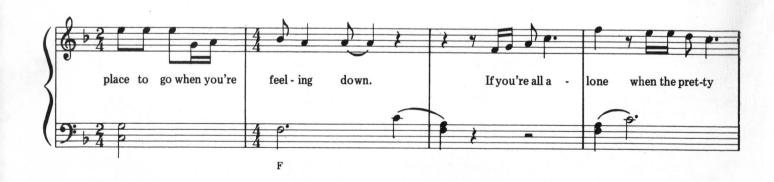

birds have flown, Ho-ney, I'm still free, take a chance on me. gon-na do my

C7

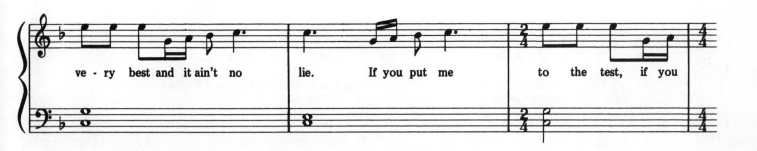

ve - ry best and it ain't no lie. If you put me to the test, if you

let me try, ___ Take a chance on me, ___ take a chance on me. ___

F   Gm   C7   Gm

___ 2. Oh you can

1. We can go dan - cing, take your time, ba - by, we can go walk - ing as I'm in no hur - ry, I

C7   Gm

long as we're to - geth - er; know I'm gon - na get you; lis - ten to some mu - sic, you don't wan - na hurt me,

F   Gm

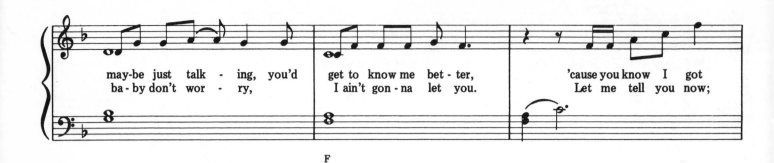

may-be just talk - ing, you'd / get to know me bet - ter, / 'cause you know I got
ba - by don't wor - ry, / I ain't gon - na let you. / Let me tell you now;

F

so much that I wan - na do. / When I dream I'm a-lone with you, it's ma - gic.__
my love is strong e - nough / to__ last when things are rough, it's ma - gic.__

Dm   Bb   Dm   Bb C

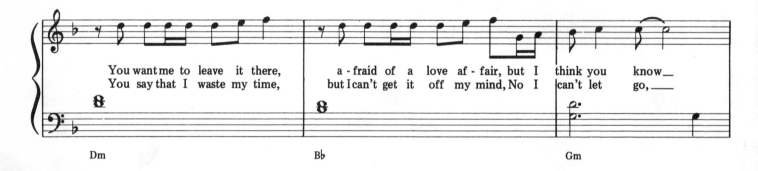

You want me to leave it there, / a - fraid of a love af - fair, but I think you know__
You say that I waste my time, / but I can't get it off my mind, No I can't let go,__

Dm   Bb   Gm

1   **2**

that I can't let go.__   If you change your
'cause I love you so.__   (me)   If you change your

C7   Gm   C   F   F

Repeat and Fade

mind,   I'm the first in / line,   Ho-ney I'm still / free,   take a chance on

C7

Why Did It Have To Be Me

Words and Music by Benny Andersson and Björn Ulvaeus

Steady Four

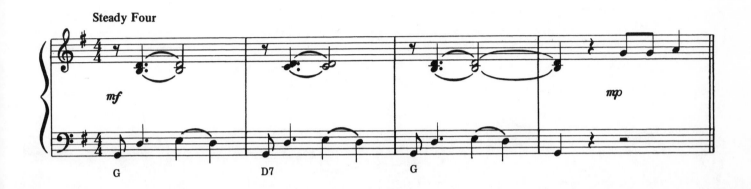

When you were lone - ly you need - ed a man, — some-one to lean — on, well

I un - der - stand, — It's on - ly na - tural, But why did it have — to be

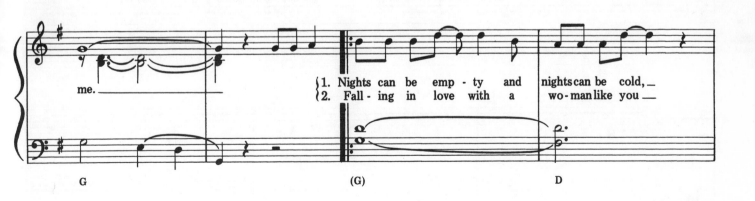

me. —
1. Nights can be emp - ty and nights can be cold, —
2. Fall - ing in love with a wo - man like you —

so you were look - ing   for some-one to hold, __   that's on - ly na - tural, But
hap-pened so quick - ly there's noth-ing to do, __   it's on - ly na - tural, But

G   D   C

why did it   have   to   be   me? ____   I was so lone-some,
why did it   have   to   be   me? ____

D7   G   G7   C

I was blue,   I could-n't help it,   it   had to be you and   I   al - ways

G   D7

thought you knew the rea - son   why.   I on - ly wan-ted a

Am7   D7   G   C

lit - tle love af - fair,   now I can see you are   be - gin - ning to care,   but

A7

ba - by   be - lieve me,   it's bet - ter

G   C   A7

to   for - get   me._____

G   D7

1

Men are the toys__ in the   game that you play;__   When you get tir - ed, you

(G)   D   G

throw them a - way,__   that's on - ly na - tural, But   why did it have__ to be

D   C   D7

Repeat and Fade

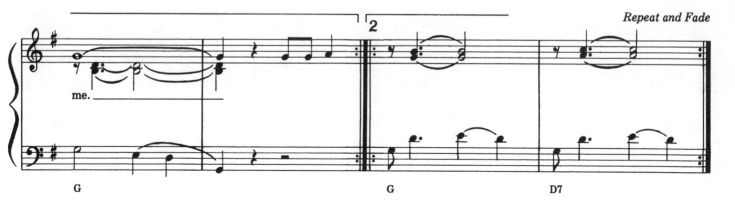

2

me._____

G   G   D7

15

Mamma Mia

Words and Music by Benny Andersson, Stig Anderson and Björn Ulvaeus

Steadily

1. I've been cheat-ed by you since I don't_ know when.
2. I've been an-gry and sad a-bout things that you do.

So I made up my mind, it must come to an end.
I can't count all the times that I've told you we're through.

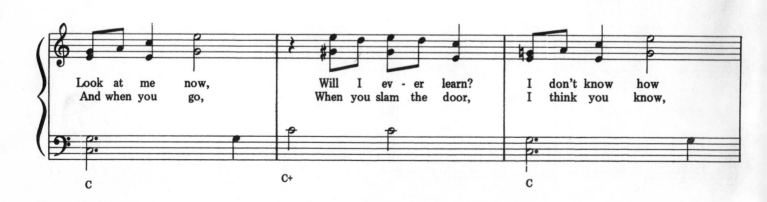

Look at me now,   Will I ev - er learn?   I don't know how
And when you go,   When you slam the door,   I think you know,

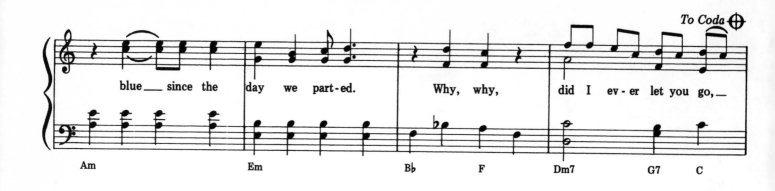

To Coda ⊕

blue___ since the day we part-ed. Why, why, did I ev-er let you go,___

Am | Em | B♭ | F | Dm7 | G7 | C

1.

Mam-ma Mi-a, now I real-ly know,___ my, my, I could nev-er let you go.___
(2.) ev-en if I say___

Am7 | B♭ | F | Dm7 | G7 | C

2.

bye, bye, leave me now or nev-er; Mam-ma Mi-a, it's a game we play,___

B♭ | F | C | Am7

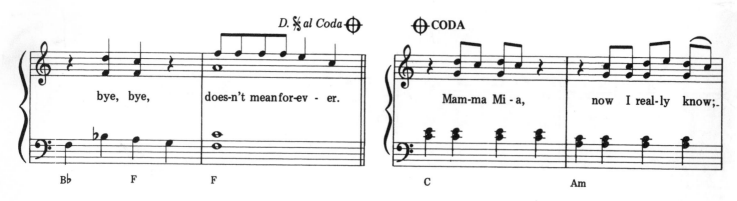

D. %& al Coda ⊕   ⊕ CODA

bye, bye, does-n't mean for-ev-er.   Mam-ma Mi-a, now I real-ly know;___

B♭ | F | F   C | Am

Repeat and Fade

my, my, I could nev-er let you go.___

B♭ | F | Dm7 | G7 | C | C

18

The Name Of The Game

Words and Music by Benny Andersson, Stig Anderson and Björn Ulvaeus

Bright Four

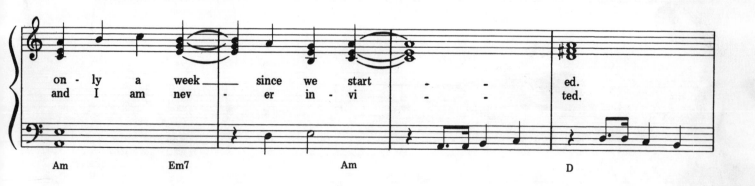

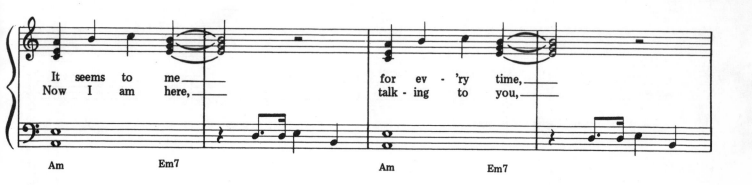

I'm get - ting more__ o - pen heart__ __ ed.
no won - der I__ get ex - ci __ ted.

Am   Em7   Am   D

I was an im - pos - si - ble case,
Your smile and the sound of your voice

No one ev - er could
And the way you see

Am   D7   Em

reach__ me,   But I think I can see in your face,
through__ me,   Got - ta feel - ing you gim - me no choice,

F   Am   D7

There's a lot you can teach__ me,__ __ So I wan - na know.
But it means a lot to__ me,__ __ So I wan - na know.

Em   F

What's the name of the game,__ does it mean an - y - thing__

G7(Csus)   C   F   G

make me show_____ what I'm try - ing to_____ con - ceal. If I

C   F   Bb   F   C7   F

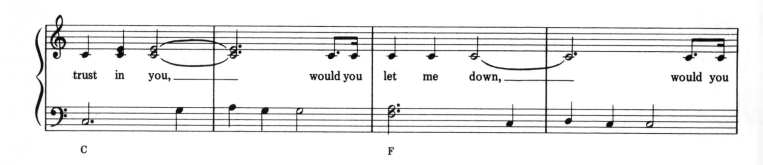

trust in you,_____ would you let me down,_____ would you

C   F

laugh at me?_____ If I said I care_____ for you,

C   Am

Could you feel the same_____ way too? I

Bm7   E   Am

wan - na know   the name of the game_____

G7(Csus)   Am   E7

Repeat and Fade

23

Honey Honey

Words and Music by Benny Andersson, Stig Anderson and Björn Ulvaeus

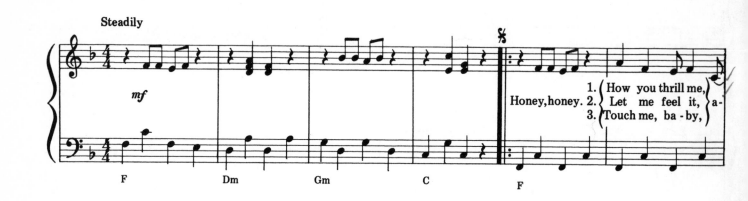

(Oh you make me diz - zy)

I don't wan-na hurt you ba-by, I

C   C   Cm7   F7

don't wan-na see you cry.— So stay on the ground girl, You bet-ter not get too high.

Bb   Gm   Cm7   F7

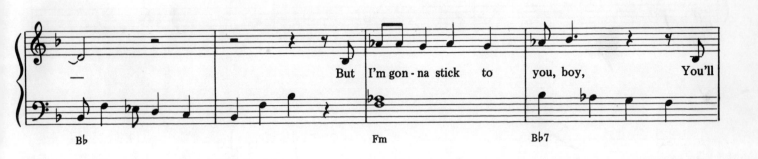

But I'm gon-na stick to you, boy, You'll

Bb   Fm   Bb7

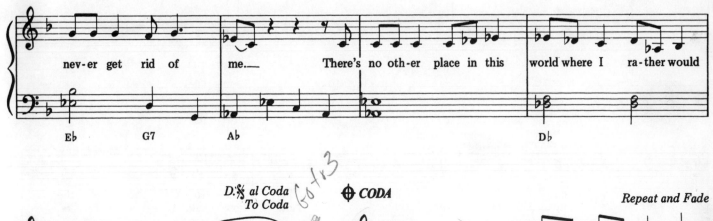

nev-er get rid of me.— There's no oth-er place in this world where I ra-ther would

Eb   G7   Ab   Db

D.S. al Coda
To Coda

CODA

Repeat and Fade

be.

beast.   (Oh you make me diz - zy)

Gm7   C7   Bb   C

Waterloo

Words and Music by Benny Andersson, Stig Anderson and Björn Ulvaeus

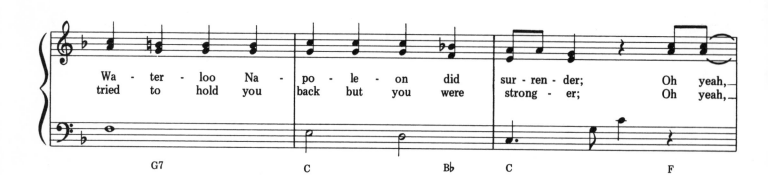

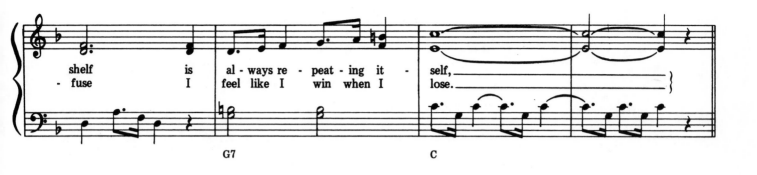

shelf   is   al‑ways re‑peat‑ing it‑self, _____
‑fuse   I   feel like I   win when I   lose. _____

G7   C

Wa‑ter‑loo,   I was de‑feat‑ed,you   won the war.

F   C7   F   Bb

Wa‑ter‑loo,   pro‑mise to love you for   ev‑er‑more.

C   F   Bb   C

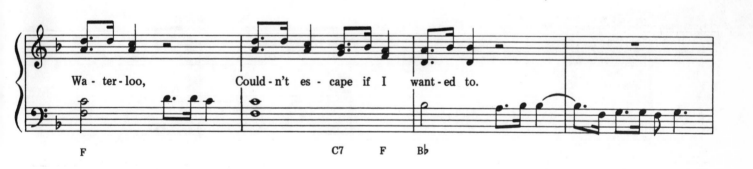

Wa‑ter‑loo,   Could‑n't es‑cape if I   want‑ed to.

F   C7   F   Bb

Wa‑ter‑loo,   Know‑ing my fate is to   be with you.   Wa, Wa, Wa, Wa,

C   F

Ring, Ring

Words and Music by Benny Andersson, Stig Anderson and Björn Ulvaeus
English lyrics by Neil Sedaka and Phil Cody

Moderato

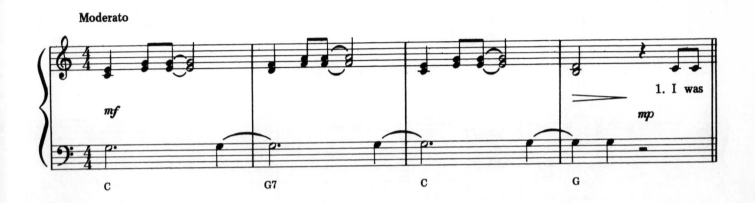

(2.) here and now you're sit-ting by the phone, gone, I was wait-ing all a-lone. Hey did I do some-thing

lone. Ba-by by my-self I sit and wait and won-der a-bout you.
wrong? I just can't be-lieve that I could be so bad-ly mis-ta-ken.

It's a dark and drea-ry night, Seems like
Was it me or was it you? Tell me

no - thing's go - ing right,   Won't you tell me ho - ney, How can
are we real - ly through?   Won't you hear me cry___ And you will

F

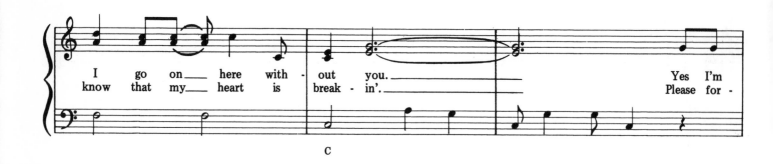

I go on___ here with - out you.___   Yes I'm
know that my___ heart is break - in'.___   Please for -

C

down and feel - in' blue,   And I don't know what___ to do;
- give and then___ for - get,   Or may - be dar - ling,___ better yet;

G   G7

Ring, ring,   Why don't you give___ me a call?___

C   G7

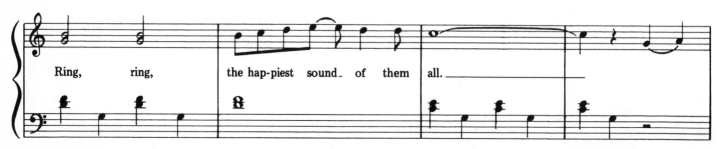

Ring, ring,   the hap - piest sound___ of them all. ___

C

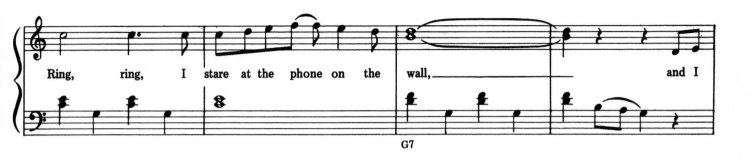

Ring, ring, I stare at the phone on the wall, and I

G7

sit all a - lone im - pa - tient - ly, Won't you please un - der - stand the

Dm

need in me, So___ Ring, ring, Why don't you give___ me a call?

G7 **C**

So, ___ Ring, ring, Why don't you give___ me a call?

G7 **C**

1

Repeat and Fade

2. You were call? So, Ring, ring, Why don't you give___ me a

2

C **G7**

Fernando

Words and Music by Benny Andersson, Stig Anderson and Björn Ulvaeus

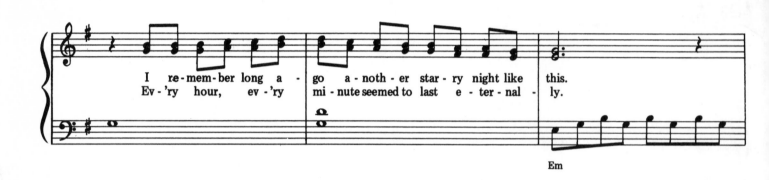

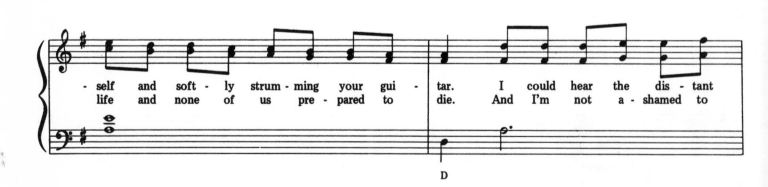

drums and sound of bu - gle calls were / say the war of guns and can - nons / com - ing from a - far.

al - most made me cry.

There was some - thing in the

air that night,— the stars were bright,— Fer - nan - do.

They were shi - ning there for you and me,— for li - ber - ty,— Fer -

- nan - do. Though we nev - er thought that we could lose. there's no re -

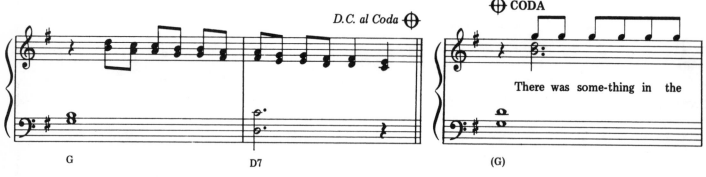

They were shi-ning there for you and me, ___ for li - ber - ty, ___ Fer -

D7   C   D7

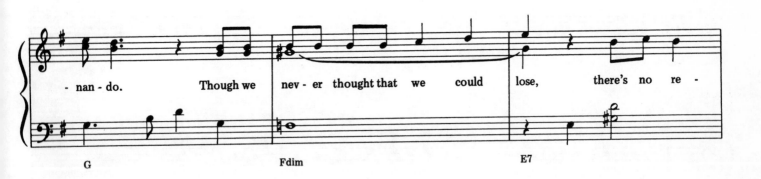

- nan - do.   Though we nev - er thought that we could lose, there's no re -

G   Fdim   E7

- gret. ___   If I had to do the same a - gain, ___   I

A7   D7   C

Repeat and Fade

would, my friend, ___ Fer - nan - do.   If I had to do the

D7   G

3. Now we're old and grey, Fernando
   And since many years I haven't seen a rifle in your hand;
   Can you hear the drums Fernando?
   Do you still recall the fateful night we crossed the Rio Grande?
   I can see it in your eyes how proud you were to fight for freedom in this land.

S.O.S

Words and Music by Benny Andersson, Stig Anderson and Björn Ulvaeus

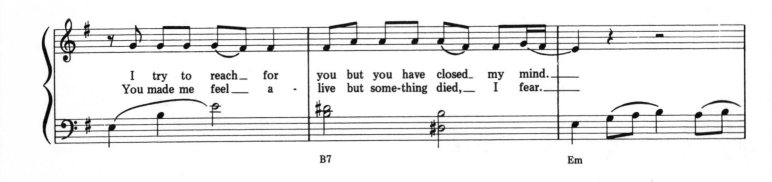

Hasta Mañana

Words and Music by Benny Andersson, Stig Anderson and Björn Ulvaeus

Fairly bright

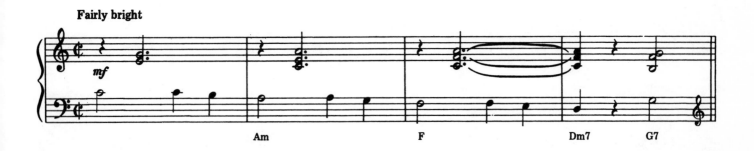

1. Where is the spring and the sum - mer,
2. Where is the dream we were dream - ing,

That once was yours and mine? _____
And all the nights we shared? _____

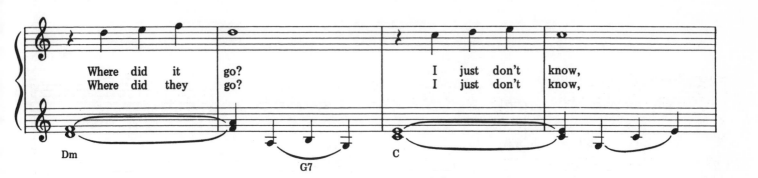

Where did it go? I just don't know,
Where did they go? I just don't know,

But still my love for you will live for - ev - er.
And I can't tell you just how much I miss you.

Dm   D7   Dm7   G7   Dm7   G7

CHORUS

Has - ta Ma - ña - na 'til we meet a - gain,____ Don't know

C   Em

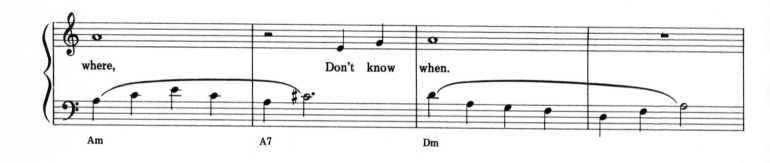

where,   Don't know when.

Am   A7   Dm

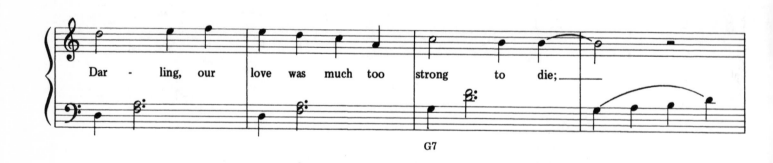

Dar - ling, our love was much too strong to die;____

G7

We'll find a way to face a new to - mor - row.

Dm   G7   Dm7   G7

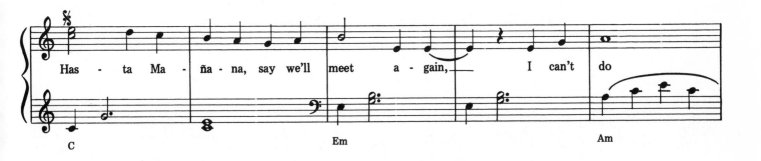

Has - ta Ma - ña - na, say we'll meet a - gain, I can't do

C   Em   Am

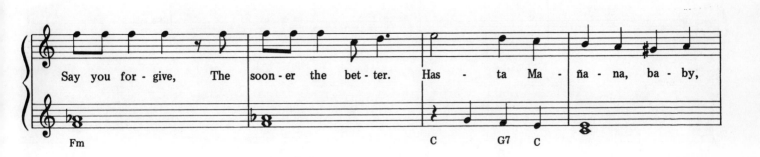

with - out you. Time to for - get, Send me a let - ter,

Dm   F

Say you for - give, The soon - er the bet - ter. Has - ta Ma - ña - na, ba - by,

Fm   C   G7   C

Has - ta Ma - ña - na, un - til then. then.

Dm   G7   C   C

D.S.   3

then.

C

Dancing Queen

Words and Music by Benny Andersson, Stig Anderson and Björn Ulvaeus

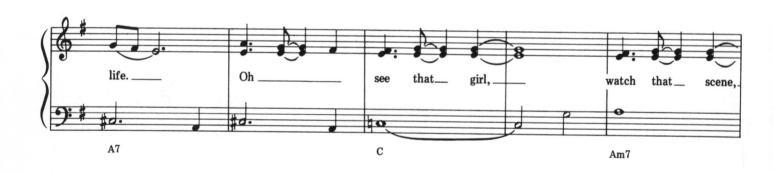

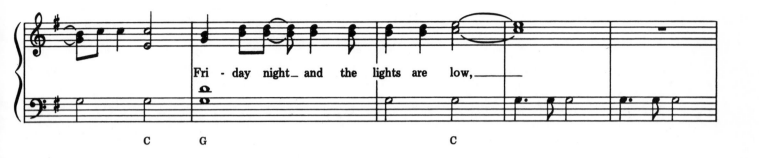

Fri - day night_ and the lights are low,

C   G   C

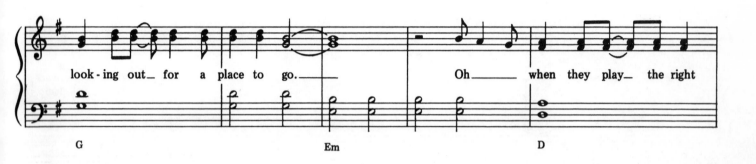

look - ing out_ for a place to go._   Oh_____ when they play_ the right

G   Em   D

mu - sic,   get - ting in _ the swing,   You come to look for a king._

G   D   G   D   Em

1. A - ny - bod - y could be that guy;_____
2. You're a tea - ser, you turn 'em on,_____

D   Em   C

night is young_ and the mu - sic's   high._____
leave 'em burn - ing and then you're gone._____

G   Em

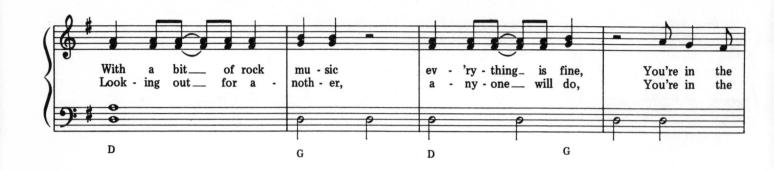

With a bit__ of rock | mu - sic | ev - 'ry - thing__ is fine, | You're in the
Look - ing out__ for a - | noth - er, | a - ny - one__ will do, | You're in the

D — G — D — G

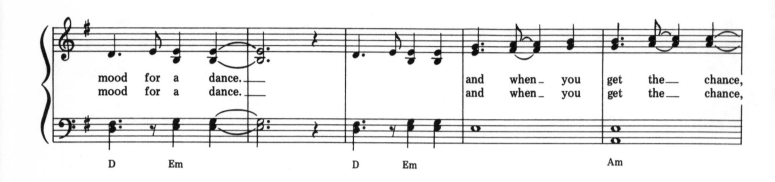

mood for a dance.__ | | and when__ you get the__ chance, |
mood for a dance.__ | | and when__ you get the__ chance, |

D — Em — D — Em — Am

| | You are__ the Dan - cing__ Queen,__ |

D — G

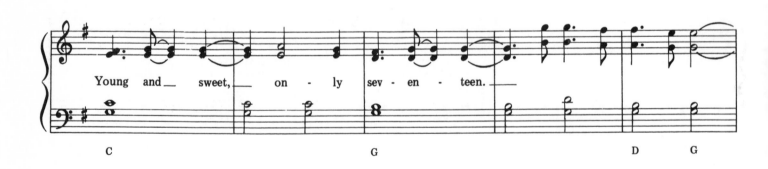

Young and__ sweet,__ on - ly sev - en - teen.__

C — G — D — G

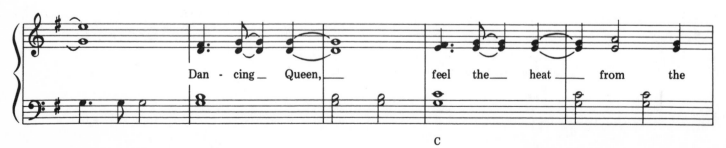

Dan - cing__ Queen,__ | feel the__ heat__ from the

C

44

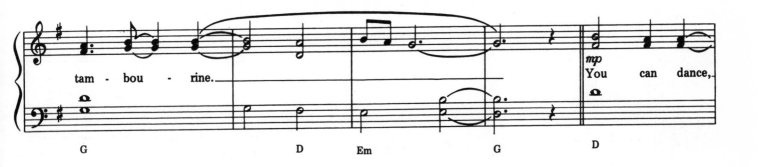

tam - bou - rine.____ You can dance,

G   D   Em   G   D

____ you can jive,____ ____ hav - ing____ the time of____ your

B7   Em

life.____ Oh____ see that____ girl,____ watch that____ scene,

A7   C   Am7

____ dig in the Dan - cing____ Queen.____

1.

G   D7   C   G   D7

Repeat and Fade

2.

Dig in the Dan - cing____ Queen,____

G   C   G   D   G

Money, Money, Money

Words and Music by Benny Andersson and Björn Ulvaeus

Moderato

mf

(no chords)

1. I work all night I work all day to
man like that is hard to find but

Am

pay the bills I have to pay,___
I can't get him off my mind,___

ain't it sad?___
ain't it sad?___

And
And

E7   **Am**

still there nev - er seems to be a
if he hap - pens to be free, I

sin - gle pen - ny left for me,___
bet he would - n't fan - cy me,___

E7

that's too bad.___
that's too bad.___

So

In my dreams___
I must leave,___

I
I'll

Am

have a plan, ___ if I got me a weal - thy man, ___ I
have to go ___ to Las Ve - gas or Mon - a - co ___ and

G   F   A7

ritard.

would - n't have to work at all, I'd fool a - round and have a ball. ___
win a for - tune in a game, my life will nev - er be the same. ___

Dm   D#dim

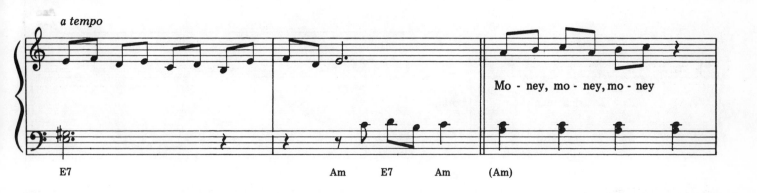

a tempo

Mo - ney, mo - ney, mo - ney

E7   Am   E7   Am   (Am)

must be fun - ny in the rich man's world.

B7   E7   Am

Mo - ney, mo - ney, mo - ney, al - way's sun - ny in the rich man's

B7   E7

world.   A - ha, _____ a - ha.

Am   Dm   E

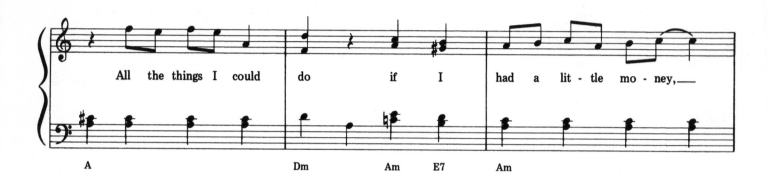

All the things I could   do   if I   had a lit - tle mo - ney,___

A   Dm   Am   E7   Am

1

it's a rich man's   world,

F   E+   Am   F7

it's a rich man's   world.   2. A

Dm   E+   Am

2

world.

Am

11/00 (38726)